Copper Work..

Rose, Augustus R. [from old catalog]

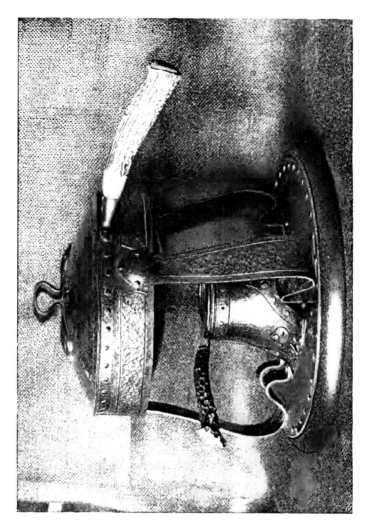

CHAFING DISH.

COPPER WORK

A Text Book for Teachers and Students
IN THE
Manual Arts

FULLY ILLUSTRATED

BY
AUGUSTUS F. ROSE
Providence Technical High School and
Rhode Island School of Design

THE DAVIS PRESS
Worcester, Massachusetts
1906

TABLE OF CONTENTS.

PREFACE.

IN this book the subject of Copper Work, as it may be introduced into the public schools, is treated to the extent of specifying an equipment and suggesting some of the possibilities of a course. Not only will there be found an abundance of illustrative material on this subject, consisting of drawings and photographs of various objects executed by upper grammar and high school pupils, but also a detailed description of the processes necessary for the execution of many of the designs. It is not expected that the problems as given will be slavishly copied, but rather that they will make clear the methods and processes that may be applied in the working out of similar problems. It is hoped that this volume will be especially helpful to teachers in the Manual Arts who are trying to introduce Metal Work into the regular school course.

The author is indebted to Charles J. Martin and Antonio Cirino, for valuable assistance in making some of the illustrations.

AUGUSTUS F. ROSE.

LIST OF ILLUSTRATIONS.

PLATE.

LIST OF ILLUSTRATIONS—(Continued).

FIGURES.

LIST OF ILLUSTRATIONS.—(Continued.)

Chapter I.

INTRODUCTION.

During the past few years many experiments have been tried in the development of Manual Training Courses and much time has been spent in discussing of what lines of work they should consist. Wood and iron were the first materials used and are yet indispensable, but experience has led those who are developing this work to believe that there are other materials as well adapted to Manual Training work in all its various forms. Clay, used not only for modeling but for ceramic work as well, leather, brass and copper are materials that have also been put to the test and found satisfactory in many ways.

In ancient times copper was known as a useful metal, and down through the ages it not only held its own but increased in usefulness. Among its valuable properties may be mentioned toughness and ductility; its toughness enables it to be beaten into thin strong sheets, while its ductility enables it to be drawn out into fine wire. Copper readily forms important alloys, such as brass from copper and zinc.

Work in sheet copper and brass has been introduced into the public school course with gratifying results. It has proved itself to be a valuable departure from other branches of Manual Training work and gives promise of being permanent. Sheet, copper and brass offer possibilities for various kinds of treatment, either in the flat work which includes saw piercing, embossing and enameling, or in the raised work.

There is something about this work that appeals to pupils and holds their interest. The nature of the material, hard enough to offer some resistance and yet pliable enough to allow its being wrought into many forms, the durability of the object when completed, and the variety of colors that may be obtained, especially with copper, all tend to make the subject not only interesting but fascinating.

All exercises in sheet metal should be of some real value to the pupil; no time should be spent on work done simply for practice, but the various steps should be learned in the making of useful objects of artistic worth. In this, as in other work, it seems best to give each member of the class the same work for a while until he has become acquainted with the different tools and learned the limitations of the material. When this has been accomplished, each pupil may be allowed to work out his own designs. In this the educational value is very greatly increased. The pupil conceives the idea and makes several sketches of it, carrying it through repeated changes until it is brought to the perfected design appropriate in every way to the idea. Some may not be fortunate enough to get a full equipment so that all of the various kinds of metal work may be done, but such may be able to make a beginning by doing light work in saw piercing, which requires a very limited equipment.

EQUIPMENT.

The equipment necessary for a start in Copper work need cost but little if the teacher is somewhat ingenious, for the patterns of the various anvils may be made by him; from these patterns the castings can be made at any foundry for three or four cents per pound. It is better to begin with a few anvils and tools and to add one or two at a time as the need is felt for a more varied supply. If the work can be done in a room already fitted with benches and vises, it will reduce the first cost considerably. Any home-made bench will do if a regulation one is not to be had. One that has given satisfaction was made of 2″ x 4″ studding with plank tops in lengths of 12 feet, giving space for

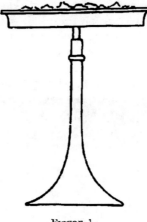

FIGURE 1.

four vises at each bench. A swivel vise that may be turned at any angle will be found satisfactory.

An annealing tray made of a piece of sheet iron in the shape of a box about 18″ square and 3″ deep, with the corners lapped and riveted and filled with slag, answers very well, but one similar to the illustration, Figure 1, is better. In

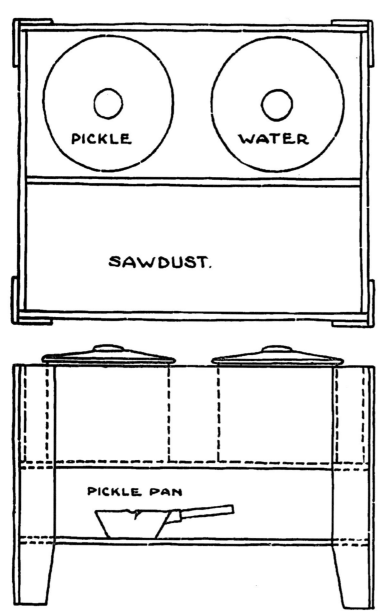

FIGURE 2.

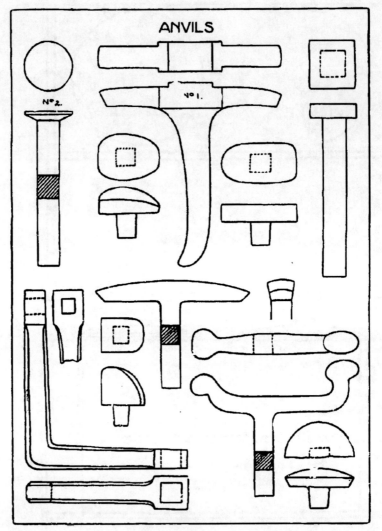

PLATE 1.

this the top is circular and rotary, which is an advantage. A pair of light long nose-tongs are needed to handle the work. Any ordinary foot bellows and blow-pipe will do.

A box, Figure 2, large enough to hold two 2-gallon stone jars and about half a bushel of sawdust, is needed. One of the jars is for water in which the object is cooled

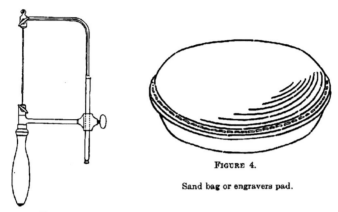

FIGURE 4.

Sand bag or engravers pad.

FIGURE 3.

after being annealed; the other is for pickle which is used to clean the work. The sawdust is used to dry the object after it has been dipped in the water.

Plate 1 illustrates forms of anvils that have been found most useful.

Plate 2 shows a variety of hammers needed.

Plate 3 shears and plyers.

The following tools are also necessary:

Cutting shears—straight and curved.
Steel square 12″.
Jeweler's saw frame. Figure 3.
Piercing saws.
Breast drill and assortment of drills.

16

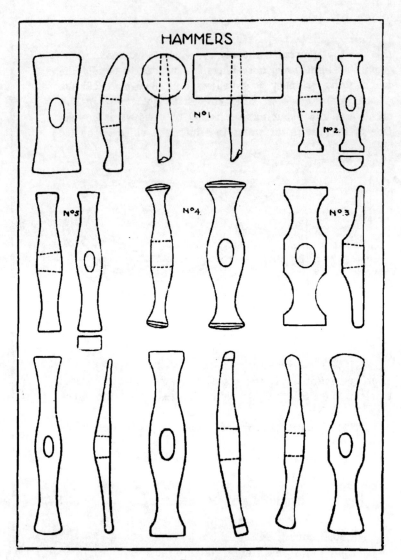

HAMMERS

No 1

No 2.

No 5

No 4.

No 3

PLATE 2.

17

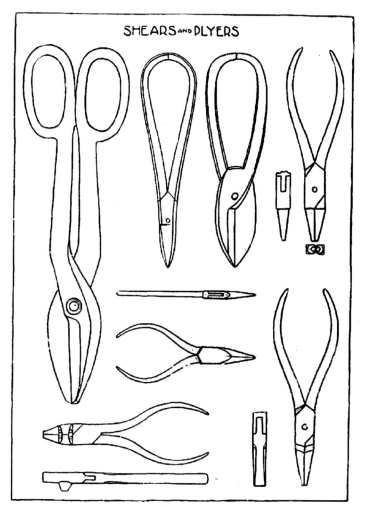

SHEARS and PLYERS

PLATE 3.

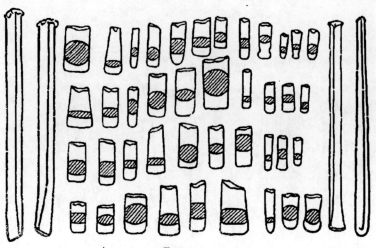

FIGURE 5.
Chasing tools and punches for embossing.

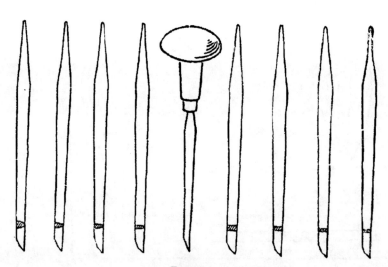

FIGURE 6.
Engraving tools.

19

Compasses.
Calipers.
Surface gauge.
Surface plate.
Assortment of files.
Sand bag or engraver's pad.   Figure 4.
Pitch block.
A set of chasing tools and punches.   Figure 5.

FIGURE 7.

A set of engraving tools.   Figure 6.
A set of dapping tools and dapping die.   Figure 7.
Plyers—flat nose, round nose, and pointed.
Cloth and felt buffs.
Borax slate.
Two 4-gallon stone crocks.
Mortar and pestle (Porcelain.)
Mouth blow-pipe.
Bench pins.

MATERIALS.

Copper is the material best suited for the work outlined in this book, although the processes as described may be applied to brass or silver. Brass may be used successfully in the flat work, but for raised work copper is the best material for the beginner.

Copper is obtainable in different thicknesses and in various grades but the best grade should be used. For most of the work from 18 to 24 gauge is used, while metal from 12 to 18 gauge is used occasionally.

Copper wire is used in several sizes for making rivets.

No. 22 and 28 iron wire is indispensable for binding when soldering.

Easy running silver solder may be made by the user, but as a small piece will solder many joints, and as it is not practical to make it in small quantities, it is better to buy it ready made as desired.

Powdered or lump borax is used as a flux in soldering. Charcoal or asbestos blocks are used when soldering small work.

Cut-quick and rouge are used for polishing.

Nitric and sulphuric acids are used to clean work.

PICKLE.

Pickle is a trade name given to solutions used in cleaning work. Different proportions of acids are used according to the work to be cleaned. For copper and silver a dilute bath of sulphuric acid is used of 1 part acid to 15 parts of water. The solution may be used cold but when used hot it becomes much more effective. When used hot a copper dish is necessary. The object being placed in the dish with enough pickle to cover it, it is then placed over a gas plate and allowed to come to boiling heat. The pickle is then poured off and the object rinsed in clean water. A dilute solution of nitric acid is used for brass.

GAUGE.

Gauge, as referred to in this book, is a term used to denote the thickness of sheet metal. The Standard Wire Gauge is divided in guage numbers from 5 to 36; and is used for measuring the thickness of wire and sheet metal. It is usually a plate of steel having round its edge a series of notches of standard openings.

Chapter II.

PROBLEMS.

ESCUTCHEONS.

Escutcheons may be made of any metal; but copper, brass, and iron are most used. The size and shape of the escutcheon are determined by the size of the lock and the space at our disposal. The outline may be circular, square

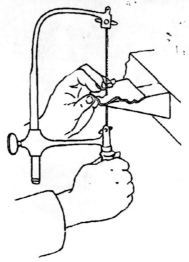

FIGURE 8.

or rectangular, or it may be modified somewhat, care being taken to keep it in harmony with its surroundings.

First make a careful drawing of the design. Take a piece of metal a little larger than the drawing calls for, and of the desired gauge, from 12 to 20 gauge is all right for such an exercise. The design is then transferred to the metal by the use of carbon paper, or a tracing is made on rice paper from the drawing and pasted on the metal. Then

ESCUTCHEONS

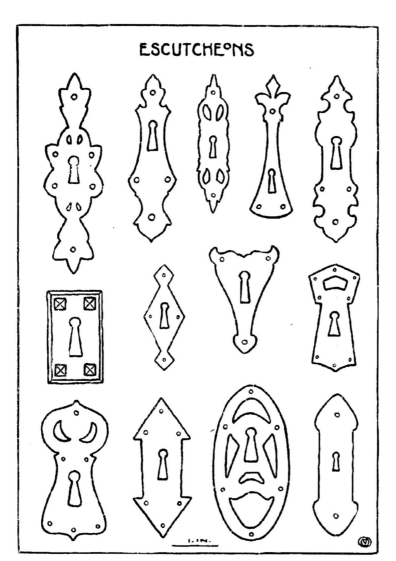

PLATE 4.

24

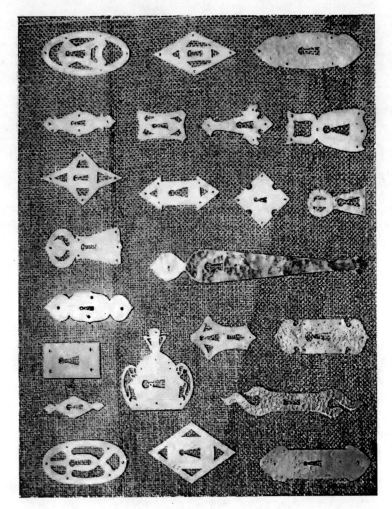

PLATE 5.

25

take a metal saw (No. 2 or 3) and saw about the design Figure 8, 8A. To saw the key whole, a hole must be drilled through which the saw can be placed to follow the line. Before drilling use a center punch, making a slight depression as a start for the drill. After the sawing is completed, a

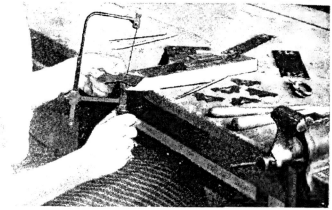

FIGURE 8 A.

file is used to true up the outline and to smooth the edges. The holes for the nails are next drilled. After using a little emery paper about the edges, it is ready to finish.

The metal, as it comes from the rolling mill, is perfectly smooth. If, in this piece of work, it is desired to make the surface a little more interesting, it may be done by taking any hammer with a smooth domed face and going over the surface. This, however, should be done before sawing. As the hammering stretches the metal somewhat, if it is left till after the sawing is done, it means more filing to get the design into shape. For a beginning this exercise has proved very satisfactory, as it gives the pupil an acquaintance with the metal and uses but a small piece of material.

HINGE TAILS.

These plates represent suggestive designs for hinges and may be given among first exercises in sawing; when so used, they should be treated like the escutcheon already described.

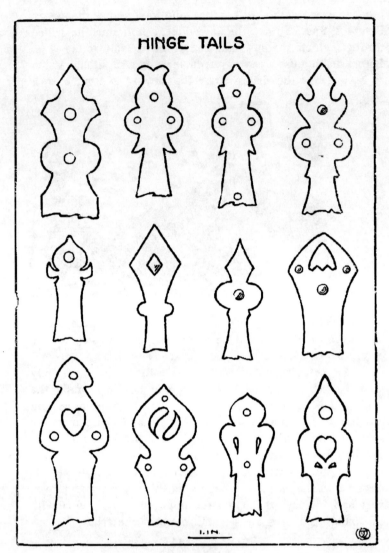

HINGE TAILS

PLATE 6.

27

HINGE TAILS

PLATE 7.

28

HINGE TAILS

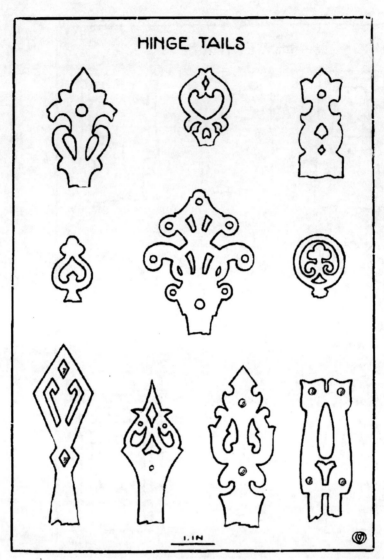

1. IN.

Plate 8.

Chapter III.

DRAWER AND DOOR PULLS.

Pulls generally consist of two parts, the handle and the plate to which the handle is fastened. Some pulls are stationary as in Figures 9, 10, while in others the handle swings from either one or two points, Figures 11, 12, 13. In this case the handle may be made by taking a rod as great

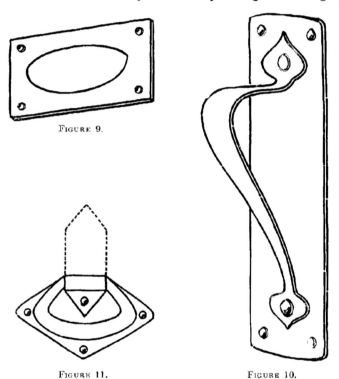

FIGURE 9.

FIGURE 11.   FIGURE 10.

in diameter as the thickest part of the handle, and either drawing it out by hammering or filing it down to the required taper. After it is tapered to the required size as at Figure

30

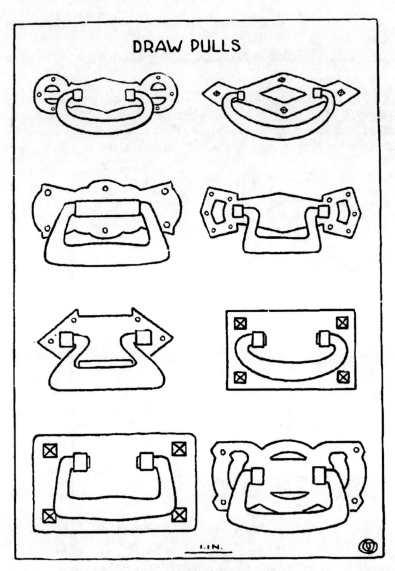

DRAW PULLS

PLATE 9.

DRAW PULLS

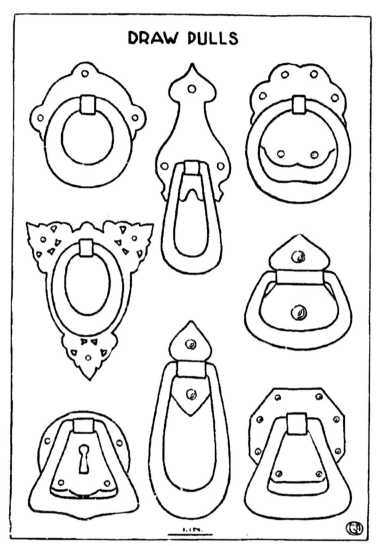

PLATE 10.

32

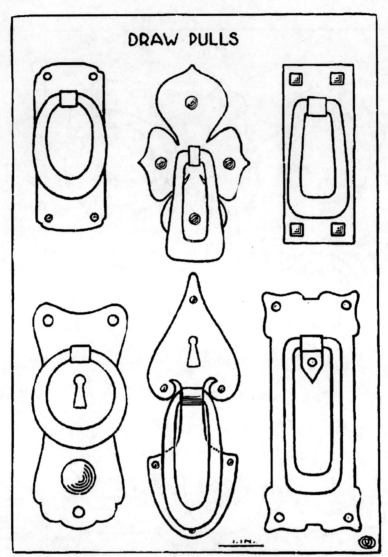

PLATE 11.

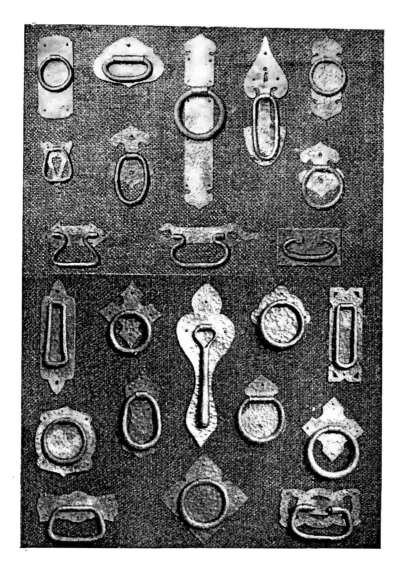

PLATE 12.

34

14, it is then bent into shape according to the design. If the handle is to swing from one or two points, it should be fastened by any one of the following methods.

Method 1. If it is possible to have the handle support go through the drawer or door, the support may be made from a

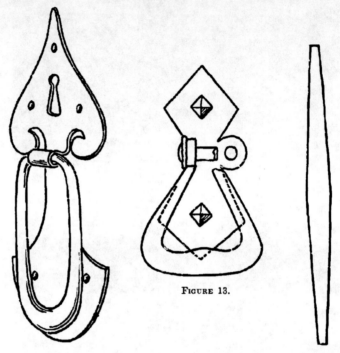

FIGURE 13.

FIGURE 12.   FIGURE 14.

piece of square rod of the length desired, a hole being drilled through one end, the size needed, as at Figure 15, A. A shoulder is then made by filing the rod down to the size of the hole in the plate. In making the shoulder the remainder of the rod which is to go through the drawer front may be left square or filed round; as the hole is round that is drilled to receive it, this last is the better way. It is also easier to

35

fasten it on the inside of the drawer when it is made in this way, for it may be simply headed up as in making a rivet, Figure 15 B, or a thread may be cut and a nut used, Figure 15 C, D. The latter method is better where taps and dies are at hand. When it is fastened by riveting, a circular or

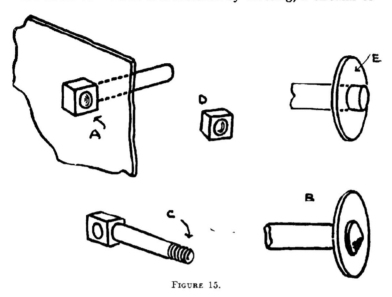

square piece of metal called a washer, Figure 15 E, a little larger in diameter than the bolt, with a hole the size of the bolt, is placed next to the drawer front on the inside; this makes the riveting more secure.

Method 2. Another method for fastening this style of a handle is to cut a slot through the plate about $\frac{1}{16}$ inch wide and length called for by the design, Figure 16 A. Then take a strip of copper in length 7 times the diameter of the handle end and as wide as the slot in the plate is long, Figure 16 B. This is then bent circular a little larger in diameter than the end of handle as at Figure 16 C, and placed in the slot as at Figure 16 D, and clinched on the back of the plate as at Figure 16 E. The plate is in this case fastened to the drawer or door by nailing or riveting.

Method 3. When it is desirable to make the plate and handle support all in one piece, it may be done in any one of three ways. First. By allowing enough metal in the center

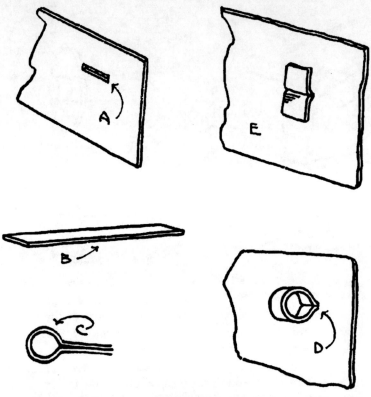

FIGURE 16.

of the plate to form the handle support as at Figure 12. Second. By allowing metal at the top of the plate to bend over handle as at Figure 11. Third. By allowing metal at the sides to be turned up at right angles to the plate to form the support as at Figure 13. In this case holes are drilled in the side pieces and a rivet is put through from one side to the other to hold the handle. For this one the handle must be either bent around the rivet or drilled to receive the rivet. In all three of these cases the plate is fastened to the door or drawer by nailing or riveting.

HINGES.

Plate 13, Various outlines of the same hinge.
Plate 14, Hinges of sameoutline with interior variations.
Plates 15, 16, 17, Butt and Strap Hinges.

In a hinge, the joint is the important feature. The size of the hinge, the strength required, and the decoration must also receive attention. After these have been determined, a drawing should be made giving a development of the joint. Whatever the size of the hinge, the following principle in regard to the joint must be kept in mind. There must be alternating projections left on the inner ends of each leaf of the hinge to fit into one another so that the pin may pass through them and allow the hinge to swing. The method of making these projections is determined by the size of the hinge.

In hinges of any considerable size, the projections are left attached to the hinge proper; in allowing for them there will be an even number on one leaf and an odd number on the other. To obtain the strength desired, the width of the projections on one leaf should equal the width of the projections on the other leaf. This applies to any number of projections. Their length should be determined by the diameter of the joint, three times the diameter is the approximate length.

In making small hinges the projections may be bent into position by the use of the round nose plyers. In larger work the projection is fastened in the vise and beginning at the end is bent around the pin a little at a time using the raw-hide mallet to work it into shape.

For small joints or hinges, such as would be used on a match box, stamp box, bon-bon box, or ink pot, the joint should be made of small tubing as described on page 100. This tubing is sawed into the required lengths and soldered to the leaves to be hinged. The parts to receive the joint are sometimes filed out.

HINGES

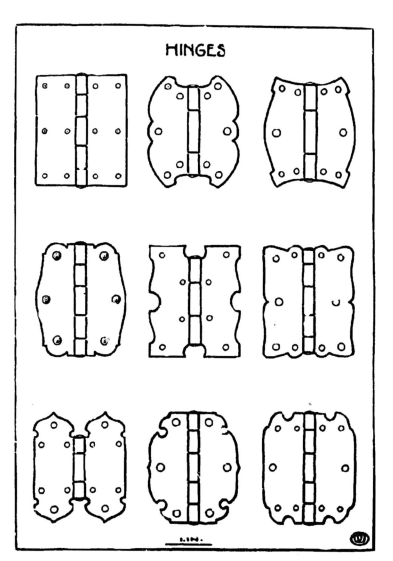

PLATE 13.

HINGES

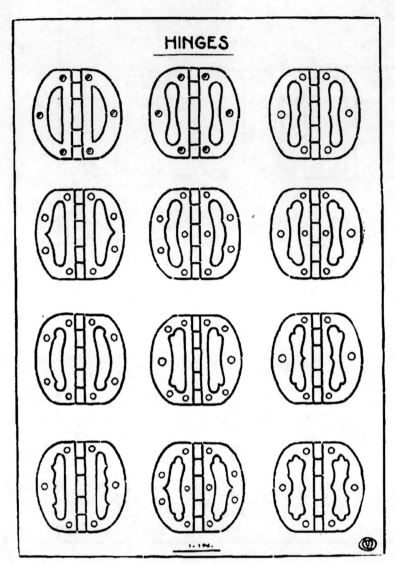

PLATE 14.

41

HINGES

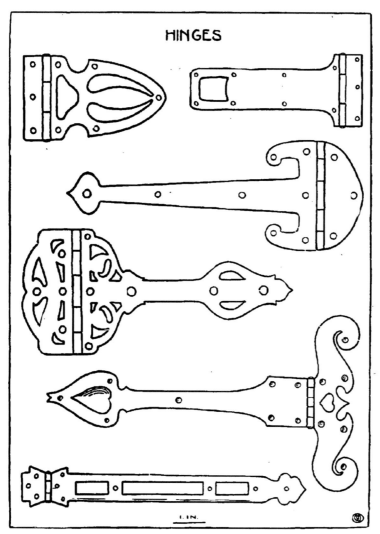

PLATE 15.

42

HINGES

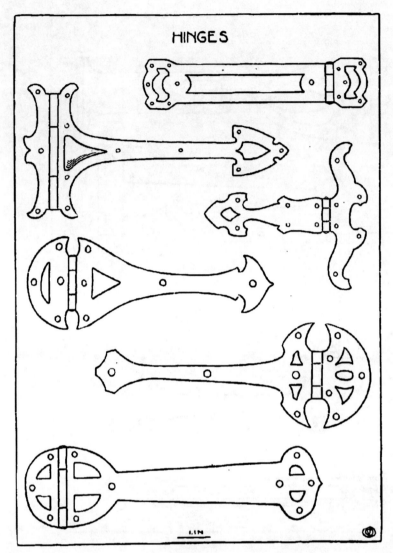

PLATE 16.

43

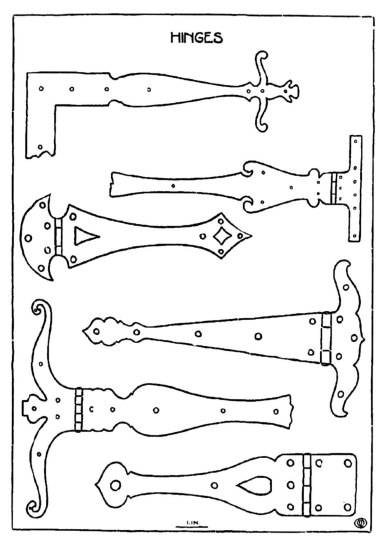

HINGES

PLATE 17.

44

Chapter IV.

FINGER PLATES.

The finger plate used on the edge of a door to receive the wear of the hand serves as an excellent exercise in sawing and filing. The design is transferred to the metal by use of carbon paper. The sawing is done as in the escutcheon. The surface may be left smooth or it may be gone over with a hammer having a face somewhat rounded. If the design calls for any repousse work, it is done as described on page 64.

PLATE 18.

46

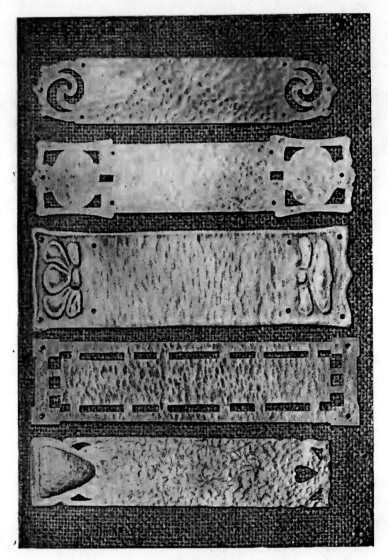

PLATE 19.

47

PAD CORNERS.

Desk pad corners while not difficult to make, are very useful as well as ornamental. The design may be carried out in any one of three ways: pierced, embossed or enameled.

In making the pattern for the pad corner, an allowance must be made for the thickness of the pad, as at A, and also for laps as at B, that are to go under the pad to hold the corners in place. The corner may be riveted to the pad at the back or the laps may be bent in such a way as to clamp them to the pad, and permit of their removal at any time.

When the design has been pierced or embossed, the laps can be bent over a piece of metal equal in thickness to that of the pad. If the design is to be carried out in enamel, all bending must be done before enameling as any expansion or contraction of the metal will crack the enamel.

DAD CORNERS

1.IN.

PLATE 20.

49

BOX CORNERS.

Box corners serve primarily to protect the corners of the box and to increase its strength, but they can be so made that they give character to the box. The corner should be designed to suit the particular box or chest to which it is to be applied. The method of making a box corner is slightly different from those previously described. After the design has been drawn, a pattern made from it in heavy paper will be found helpful, for this pattern may be used to mark out the design on the metal. In this way irregularities in the design are less likely to occur than when the design is transferred with the carbon paper directly to the metal. The decoration may be pierced or embossed, according to one's choice. After the sawing or embossing has been done, it should be filed carefully and smoothed up with fine emery cloth to do away with crude and sharp edges.

The holes for the rivets are then drilled and the burr that is made by drilling is removed with a larger drill. The two edges, A A. Plate 21, that are to come together when in place on the box should be beveled a little so that they will form a better corner. After this is done, the sides are bent down over a block of wood or metal placed in the vise. A rawhide hammer should be used to avoid marks on the face of the corner. In this as in other work, if it is desired that the metal have a hammered surface, the effect must be given before the design is cut out.

Suitable rivets are next made as described on page 98 and illustrated on page 99. After being colored or polished the corner is ready to be applied to the box.

BOX CORNERS

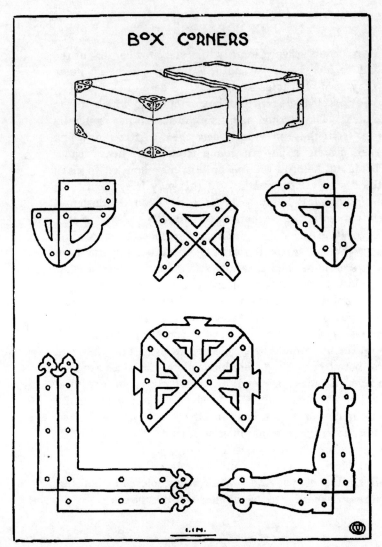

PLATE 21.

51

BOX CORNERS

PLATE 22.

STAMP BOXES.

Stamp boxes may be made in various ways, three of which are described below:

Box No. 1 and 2, Plate 23.

On a piece of 20 gauge metal, lay out or draw the pattern as shown on the plate; first with pencil, then with a scratch awl to insure permanency, going over the lines lightly on

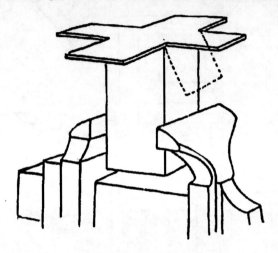

FIGURE 18.

the metal. By the use of a saw frame and a No. 3 saw the corners of the square are cut out.

The edges that form the corners are next filed up, keeping all edges straight and at right angles; after this, the edges are beveled a little, forming a mitre which, when soldered, makes a better joint than otherwise.

The sides are next bent up over an iron block placed in the vise as at Figure 18. The corners should be brought well together, using a rawhide hammer, No. 1, Plate 2.

A piece of iron wire about No. 24 is then placed around the box and twisted tight enough to hold the corners in

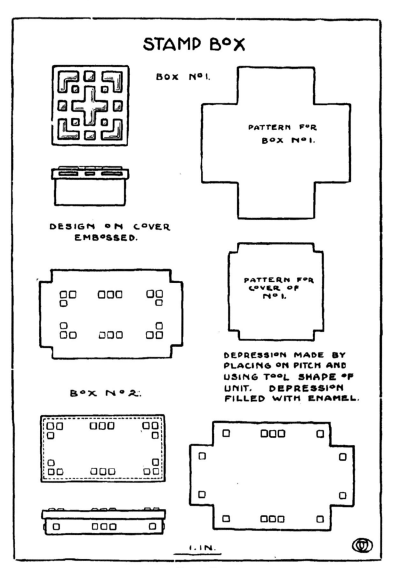

PLATE 23.

place while being soldered, Figure 19. Borax and solder are next applied and the soldering done as described on page 63. In this case, however, all of the corners should be prepared at the same time for soldering. If but one corner is prepared and soldered, the heat necessary for soldering causes the copper oxides to come to the surface at the other corners which must be removed before they can be soldered. This is remedied by coating with borax and placing the solder at all corners before applying any heat.

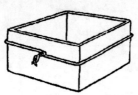

FIGURE 19.

FIGURE 20.

After the soldering is done the box is pickled. Surplus solder is next removed by filing. The box is again placed over the iron block which is held in the vise; the corners and bottom edges are squared up, using the round end of hammer shown at No. 2, Plate 2, and the top is filed off level. This completes the body part of the box.

The cover is made in the same way as the box. Much care must be taken to have the pattern carefully and accurately drawn so that when the cover is finished it will fit closely to the body. The design, if there is any, whether it is embossed or enamelled, must be carried out before cutting it to size.

Box No. 2, although of different proportion, is made in the same way as No. 1.

Box No. 3, Plate 24.

Take a strip of metal as wide as the required depth of the box and as long as the sum of the four sides. The length of each side is measured off on this strip and a line

55

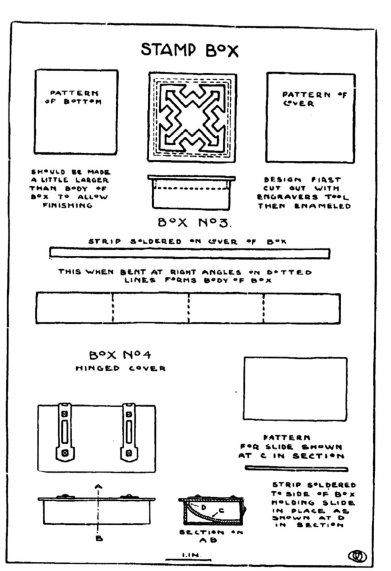

STAMP BOX

PATTERN OF BOTTOM

PATTERN OF COVER

SHOULD BE MADE A LITTLE LARGER THAN BODY OF BOX TO ALLOW FINISHING

DESIGN FIRST CUT OUT WITH ENGRAVERS TOOL THEN ENAMELED

BOX Nº3.

STRIP SOLDERED ON COVER OF BOX

THIS WHEN BENT AT RIGHT ANGLES ON DOTTED LINES FORMS BODY OF BOX

BOX Nº4

HINGED COVER

PATTERN FOR SLIDE SHOWN AT C IN SECTION

STRIP SOLDERED TO SIDE OF BOX HOLDING SLIDE IN PLACE AS SHOWN AT D IN SECTION

SECTION ON AB

B

1.IN.

PLATE 24.

PLATE 25.

scratched at right angles to the edge. The strip is then placed over a block of metal and, with a rawhide hammer bent at right angles at scratched lines, making three corners, leaving the ends to meet at the fourth corner where they are to be soldered. These ends should be mitered as in Box 1, before soldering. After the corner has been soldered and the box pickled, it is again placed over a block and trued up square. Having decided which is to be the top and which the bottom of the box, file the bottom edges level and at right angles to the sides. A piece of metal is then cut for the bottom large enough to allow about $\frac{1}{16}''$ to project on all four sides.

It is then prepared for soldering and bound together with iron wire, Figure 20. The solder should be cut in small pieces and placed about the inside edges. In soldering the bottom, care must be taken not to unsolder the corner. This may be avoided by keeping the flame away from the soldered corner until the rest of the solder has run, applying it to the corner at the last and only for a fraction of a minute.

After the soldering, the box is pickled and the edges of the bottom filed square. The $\frac{1}{16}''$ that was allowed to project may be filed flush with the sides of the box or left to project a little.

The cover is made by taking a strip of metal about $\frac{3}{16}''$ wide and long enough to fit around the inside of the box. The length of the sides (inside measurement) is laid out and then bent over a block as previously described. The corner is soldered and the upper edges are filed off level and soldered to a piece of metal, forming the top. This strip on the inside keeps the cover in place. If the design on the cover is to be carried out in enamel it should be done after the cover is completed. If the design is to be embossed, it should be done before the strip which holds the cover in place is soldered on.

PLATE 26.

59

Box No. 4, Plate 24.

The body of this box may be made like either No. 1 or No. 3. An addition is shown on this one which allows the stamp to be taken from the box more easily. A strip of 20 gauge metal $\frac{1}{16}$" wide is soldered on the inside next to the top edge extending from one end to the other as shown in the section at D. Another piece of the same gauge metal is cut, in length equal to the inside length of the box and about $\frac{1}{4}$" wider than the box. This is placed inside the box and sprung into place as shown at C in the section. This device may be applied to either of the other boxes.

The cover of this box is made of but one piece and hinged with a strap hinge, which also forms the cover decoration.

To give the surface of the metal of this box a bold hammered surface adds much to its attractiveness.

MATCH BOX.

The Match Box may be made in the same way as the Stamp Box with the exception of the cover. It seems better to have the cover of the match box hinged. The hinge may be made so as to form a part of the decoration of the cover by making it a strap hinge as shown at Plates 15, 16, 17. The hinge may also be made of tubing and extend across the back of the box. This method leaves the cover to be decorated in some other way, either by embossing or by enameling or by both.

MATCH BOX

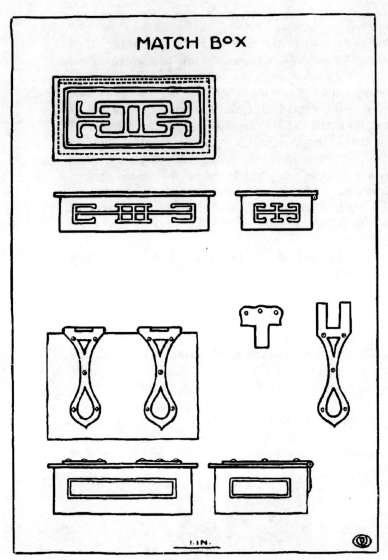

PLATE 27.

61

Plate 28.

62

Chapter V.

SCONCE A.

The pattern for this sconce as shown at Plate 29A is transferred to the metal which is then cut out. The part which serves as a reflector is raised by placing the metal face down on a sand bag, or on pitch and with the pein end of a chaser's hammer or with a pointed horn hammer, driving the center down to the required depth. If the face is somewhat irregular, it can be trued up by placing it on a block of wood and going over it with a rawhide hammer.

The shelf on which the candle socket rests is formed by bending the lower part of the sconce at right angles as shown by the dotted line. The projections at 2, 3, 4, Plate 29A, when bent into shape as shown on Plate 29 form the supports for the candle socket. The projection at 5 Plate 29A when bent into shape serves as a bracket to support the shelf. The candle socket is made from a strip of metal bent into cylindrical shape with the ends riveted together. When the socket has been riveted and holes drilled as indicated, the sconce is finished according to taste and mounted on a back of wood stained to harmonize with the color of the metal.

SCONCE A.

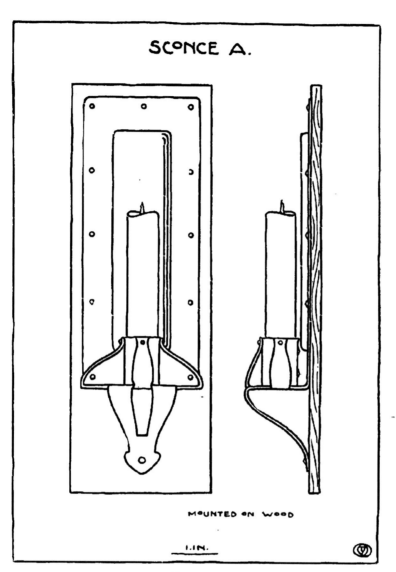

MOUNTED ON WOOD

1.IN.

PLATE 29.

64

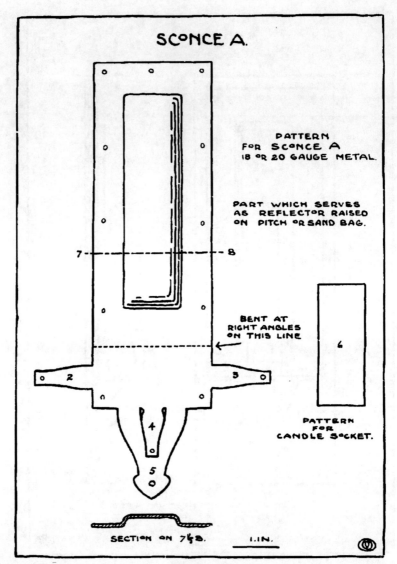

SCONCE A.

PATTERN
FOR SCONCE A
18 OR 20 GAUGE METAL.

PART WHICH SERVES
AS REFLECTOR RAISED
ON PITCH OR SAND BAG.

7 ---------- 8

BENT AT
RIGHT ANGLES
ON THIS LINE

6

PATTERN
FOR
CANDLE SOCKET.

SECTION ON 7 & 8.   1.IN.

PLATE 29 A.

65

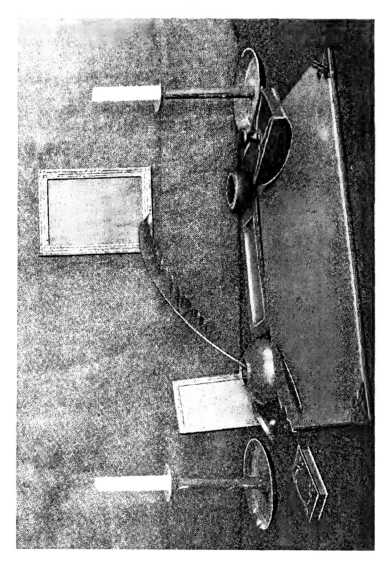

. Plate 30.

66

SCONCE B.

A rectangular piece of metal is cut out about $\frac{1}{2}$ inch larger on all sides than the design calls for and given a hammered surface with the pein end of a large hammer. After the design has been transferred to the back of the metal, it is then placed on pitch face down, and with a suitable tool the lines are sunk at A and B, Plate 31, about $\frac{1}{16}''$, as shown in the section at C. It is then removed from the pitch and, after cleaning, is put over a sand bag face up, and with a rawhide hammer, the part that is to serve as a reflector is concaved a little.

The candle socket is made like the pattern as shown at D. It is bent cylindrical in shape and the ends are riveted together, then the laps on either side are bent nearly at right angles and serve to hold the socket in place. The cup is made from a circular piece of metal hammered into a slightly conical shape, E. A rod the length required is bent at right angles with a shoulder left at each end. The bracket is made next like the pattern F and bent into shape as at G.

When all the parts are finished, they are put together. Place the rod in a vise with the short end up. The cup is put over the pin at H, and also the socket, so that the pin passes through the holes in both laps. The pin is then headed up, holding all securely in place. The bracket is next riveted to the back at K, through which the rod is put, the pin passing through the back is headed up at L. After finishing, the sconce may be mounted on a wood back.

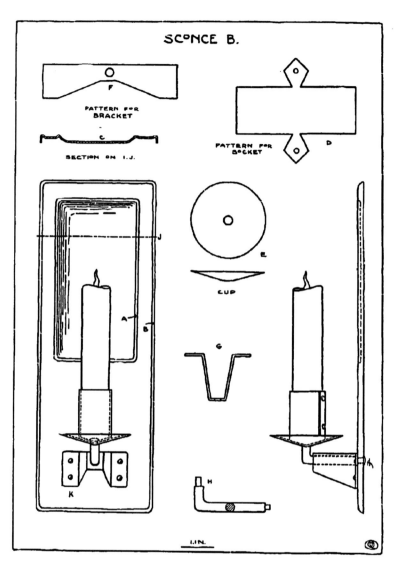

SCONCE B.

PATTERN FOR
BRACKET

SECTION ON I.J.

PATTERN FOR
SOCKET

CUP

PLATE 31.

PICTURE FRAME.

This object is made as follows: Take a piece of metal quite a little larger than the outline of the frame that is to be made. Draw on this piece of metal the outline of the frame and also the extensions which are folded back to give the thickness necessary for the reception of the picture, glass, and back, as shown at B. Have the side opposite to that on which the drawing is done free from scratches as it is to serve later as the front. Any decoration that is used must be of the simplest sort. This decoration may be pierced or in repousse. The frame here illustrated and the plate of designs were intended for repousse as more satisfactory results have been obtained by this process. After the design for the decoration of the front of the frame has been transferred to the same side of the metal as the outline, it must be prepared for the repousse process. This is done by placing it on a pitch pot. The pitch is softened enough so that the metal will stick to it. After placing the metal on the pitch, work a little of the pitch over the edges as this will hold it more securely. It is then allowed to cool or harden before working. With a suitable tool and hammer, after the pitch is hard, follow the lines which make up the design or decorative part of the frame. The lines should be gone over lightly, slowly, and carefully at first until the design is fairly well started; then they may be gone over again, sinking them a little deeper each time until they have been carried deep enough to give the design the required relief on the face of the frame. For this part of the work the tool should not be used as a punch, driving the metal down in one place and then moving it to another and so on, but it should be kept moving all the time and should at the same time receive a repeated number of light blows from the hammer. By so doing the face of the work will be smooth, otherwise each blow from the hammer will show.

PICTURE FRAME

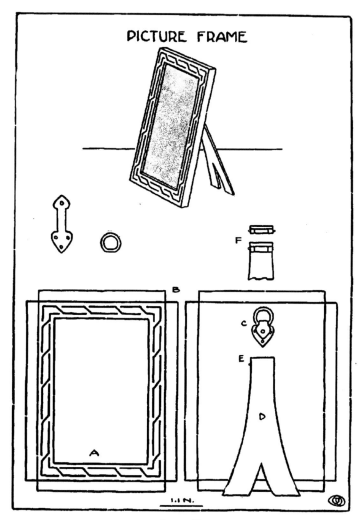

PLATE 32.

70

If there is doubt as to the depth to which the lines should be carried, the work may be taken off the pitch occasionally, so that the face may be seen. It is not an easy thing to reduce relief in this work, therefore it is better to go carefully working it up slowly. After the repousse part of the frame is done, clean it with kerosene and pickle.

The corners may then be cut out as at B, filed up square, and beveled as in the box. The sides are then bent back over a block of wood or metal, bringing the corners well together. They are then soldered. A metal saw is used to make the opening, A, the edges of which are then filed up square.

The back for this frame is made in the same way as the front except that it is left perfectly plain. This should be made to fit inside of the frame tight enough so that no fastening will be needed to hold it in place.

A frame of this size and kind may be made to hang or to stand. If it is to hang, a small ring may be made and fastened to the back as shown at C. If it is to stand, a support of some kind such as is shown at D is needed. This is made of the same thickness metal as the frame and may be made in many outlines. This support may be made stationary by riveting it to the back, or hinged, which is much better, as is shown at E and F. The hinge is made by taking a piece of about $\frac{1}{8}''$ tubing and cutting three pieces, making one of the pieces equal in width to the other two and having the three equal in width to the top of the support. The two short pieces are soldered to the back and the long piece to the support. A piece of wire equal in diameter to the hole in the tube is then cut and put in place which hinges the back and support together.

The method of making the tubing used for the above is described on page 100.

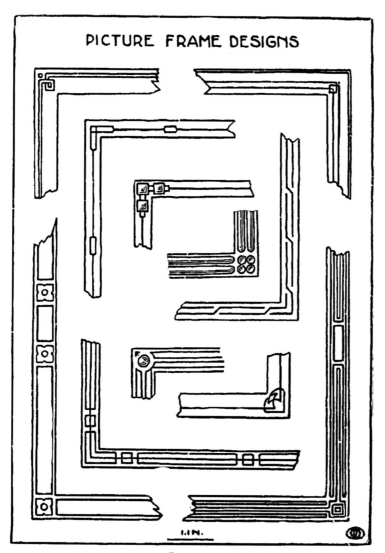

PICTURE FRAME DESIGNS

PLATE 33.

72

SOLDERING.

A piece of silver solder, a slate slab such as is ordinarily used for grinding ink, powdered or lump borax, and a soft hair brush of some sort are all that is necessary for the process of soldering in addition to what we already have.

The pieces of metal that are to be soldered must be absolutely free from all foreign matter. To insure this the joint is scraped bright with some sharpe-edged tool. Care must be taken to keep the fingers away from the joint as any moisture or greasy substance will prevent the solder from running. The best results are obtained only by being extremely careful as to cleanliness throughout the process. Being sure that the slab is perfectly clean, a little water is put in it and the lump of borax is ground around until the water becomes like thin cream. If powdered borax is used a block of wood will answer as a pestle to grind the borax to the right consistency.

The solder may be obtained any gauge, but about 20 answers for most purposes. After cutting the solder into pieces about $\frac{1}{8}$ of an inch long and about the same width, drop them into the borax that has been ground to give them a coating of borax and to remove any grease that may have adhered to them. Coat the surfaces that are to be soldered with the borax being careful to get no more borax about than is necessary. Put the parts together and bind them with No. 24 iron wire, not too tightly. The pieces of solder are then lifted with the brush used for the borax or with a pair of tweezers and placed next to the edge that is to be soldered, about one inch apart. The object is then placed on the annealing tray, which answers for soldering as well, and with the blow-pipe it is heated, very slowly at first until the water has evaporated and the borax crystallized and dissolved, the flame may then be applied more directly and the object brought to a soldering heat. If the heat is applied

73

too quickly, it will throw off the solder; and if heated hotter than necessary it is liable to melt or burn the parts being soldered, so the process demands the closest attention from the start.

The object is then pickled, washed in clear water and dried in the sawdust.

If the above directions are carefully followed good results may be expected.

REPOUSSE OR EMBOSSING.

Repousse or embossing involves practically the same principle as modeling in clay or wax, the only difference being that metal is used as the material and that different tools are employed. In this, as in clay or wax work, it is desirable to bring certain parts of a design into relief; to do this with metal the work must be placed on a substance which will give some resistance and yet allow each blow of the hammer or tool to make an impression. The substance commonly used for this purpose has the following composition, in the proportions given:

Black pitch	1 lb.
Tallow	3 teaspoonfuls.
Plaster of Paris	½ cup.

The pitch is put in some kind of dish (agate is good), placed over a gas plate, and melted. The tallow is then added and the plaster sprinkled and stirred in, the whole being well mixed. It is then poured into the pitch pot, or whatever it is to be used in. When used in hot weather more plaster must be used. A pot, hemispherical in shape, Figure 21, made of cast iron about ½ inch thick is generally used. This, when placed on a chaser's pad or ring, Figure 21, may be turned at any angle, and is found to be a great convenience. An ordinary 7" x 12" baking pan of iron

74

serves the purpose, or a box may be made of wood, but of course this is not so durable.

After allowing the composition to cool partly, yet while soft enough to stick, the piece of work that is to be embossed is placed on it, the right side next to the pitch. It is then allowed to cool still more; when quite hard or when it is difficult to make an impression on it with the thumb nail, it is ready to work on. The design is next drawn or transferred to the metal by the use of carbon paper and then scratched on with a scratch awl to make the drawing more permanent, as in going over the piece of work the pencil or carbon lines are easily erased.

The tools necessary for this work may be made as needed according to each individual design. There are a few general ones that are always found useful, such as those shown at Figure 5. Figure 22 shows a hammer generally used for this work.

FIGURE 21.

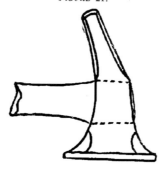

FIGURE 22.

76

Chapter VI.

RAISED FORMS.

The first exercise in raising should be a form quite simple in outline, Plate 34 A. A drawing or blue print should be used showing the shape and dimensions and this should be worked to as closely as possible. Next select a piece of copper suitable in thickness for an object of this size, in this case 20 gauge. The metal for raising must be circular in shape and the diameter of the piece needed for this bowl determined in the following way:

Take a piece of string, place it on the drawing or blue print, starting in the center of the base, and follow the curve as indicated at A, on Plate 34. This will give the radius needed for describing the circle, which is $5\frac{1}{2}''$. The circle is then cut out with the shears, after which another circle is described on the metal for the base. All lines made on the metal should be made quite lightly.

As a rule the copper comes from the rolling mill somewhat hardened so the next thing to do is to soften it by a process called annealing.

Place upon the annealing tray, Figure 1, the circular piece of metal already cut, and apply the flame from the blow-pipe upon it until it becomes red hot. It is either allowed to cool off gradually or dipped in cold water and then dried in the sawdust.

Select an anvil the shape of which conforms somewhat to the outline of the bowl and also to the curve of the base. It is often necessary to use several anvils to complete an object, but a little experience will help to decide which should be used first. The No. 1 anvil on Plate 1 seems to be about what is needed for this particular piece of work.

The anvil is placed in the vise and the metal held in the left hand against the anvil so that the end of the anvil

RAISED FORMS

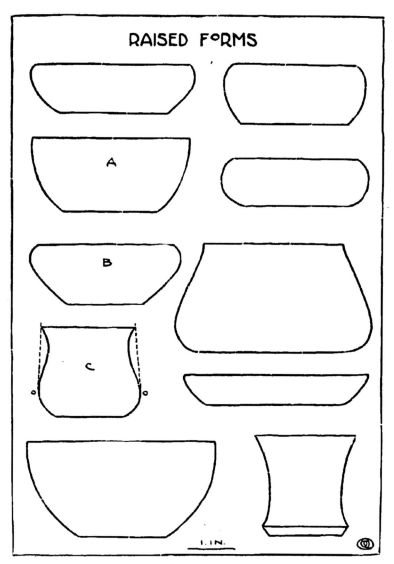

PLATE 34.

78

FIGURE 23.

comes directly under the circle which represents the base, as shown at Figure 23. With a raising hammer, No. 3 on

FIGURE 24.

Plate 2, begin hammering with light blows at first, following the circle closely the first time around until the base is well

79

started. This operation is continued at each turn striking a little above the previous blows until the top is reached when it will take the shape as shown at Figure 24. Sometimes a horn or box-wood mallet is used to start a piece of work. As the hammering hardens the metal it is necessary to anneal it each time after going over the surface. After this is done, we proceed as at first until the required form is obtained as called for by the drawing.

Care must be taken not to stretch the metal any more than can be helped as the more it is stretched the thinner it becomes.

The surface and outline of the bowl left by the raising hammer is quite irregular and needs to be trued up by a process called planishing; for this a No. 2 or 4 hammer, Plate 2, with a polished face and somewhat broader than the raising hammer is used. By going over the surface with this hammer all irregularities are removed leaving a refined curve and a finished surface.

If the bottom gets a little out of shape during the operation of raising, it can be easily brought back again by using a No. 2 stake, Plate 1, and a No. 5 hammer, Plate 2.

During the raising process the top edge has also become very irregular and must now be trimmed off level. Place the bowl on some level surface (a surface plate will give the best results) and with the point in the surface gauge describe a line about the top making it the desired height, Figure 25. A small pair of shears is then used to trim off the top to the line, after which a file is used to finish the edge, leaving it perfectly smooth. A piece of fine emery cloth may be used at the last.

The principle of raising as here described applies to forms of all sorts with few variations. Where a form is to be raised with the top edge turned in as at B, Plate 34, an anvil similar to the outline must be used. In raising a form like C, Plate 34, the sides are carried up as shown by

PLATE 35.

81

the dotted lines and then the form is reversed and the neck part drawn in. A deep form is raised more quickly if, at the start, the metal is placed on a crinkling block and the edge crinkled.

FIGURE 25.

In all raised work after one becomes acquainted with the material, it will be found that the metal can be forced in any direction, giving thickness at the bottom, at the sides, or at the rim, as is necessary.

After raising a form like C, Plate 34, it may be desired to increase the diameter a little at o-o, where an anvil

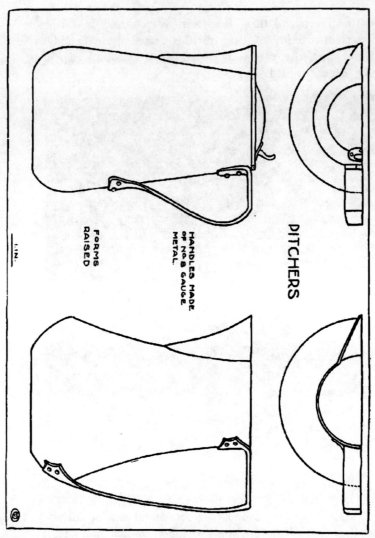

PITCHERS

HANDLES MADE
OF No.8 GAUGE
METAL.

FORMS
RAISED

PLATE 36.

83

cannot be used; or, if the form is satisfactory it may be
necessary to raise certain parts of it to carry out the decoration called for by the design. This is done by the use of
the snarling-iron, made as illustrated at Figure 26, which
shows the general outline only, as the ends vary in form

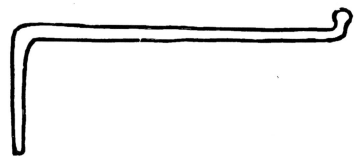

FIGURE 26.

according to the work they are to do. One arm of the iron
is held in the vise as at Figure 27. The form is then placed
over the end and held with the left hand while, with a
hammer in the right hand, the iron is struck quite near
the end in the vise which causes the other end to rebound.
This serves the same purpose as a direct blow from a hammer, except that it works much more slowly.

FIGURE 27.

85

PLATE 37.

86

PLATE 38.

87

Chapter VII.

PORRINGER.

The making of a porringer serves as a very interesting exercise; and it is so simple in form that it can be raised after very little experience. A suitable handle must also be designed, sawed out and soldered to the body.

After the bowl has been raised into shape according to the design, the top is cut and filed off level. When the handle has been sawed out and the edges trued up, it is fitted to the bowl part. Mark on the edge of the bowl the place where the handle is to be fitted and fit it at that

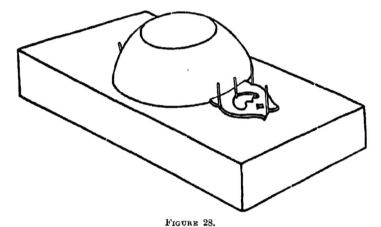

FIGURE 28.

place. The edge of the bowl where the handle is to be soldered should be filed or scraped bright before the soldering process is begun.

Invert bowl and handle and lay them upon a level block of charcoal, as shown at Figure 28. Four or five wire nails or pieces of iron wire forced into the charcoal keep the handle and bowl together. The borax is applied and sufficient solder to make a good joint. Use no more solder

88

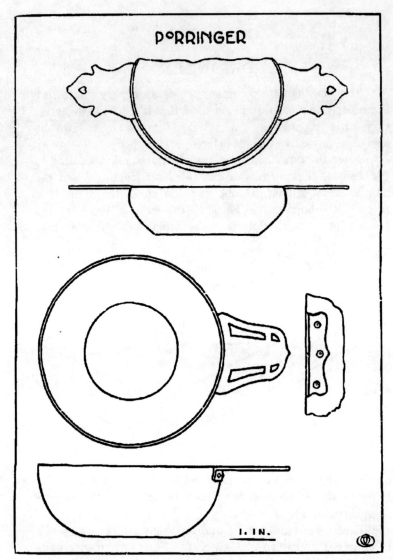

PORRINGER

I. IN.

PLATE 39.

PORRINGER HANDLES

PLATE 40.

90

than is necessary, as it will have to be removed by filing and the less filing that is done about such a joint the better the work will be. After the exercise has cooled, it may be pickled, washed and dried.

While the heat is being applied for soldering, the bowl is at the same time annealed and becomes so soft that it is easily bent out of shape. The bowl of course must be hardened again; this is done by placing it on an anvil that conforms to the outline of the bowl and hammered lightly over the surface. The handle is also treated in the same way.

Any necessary filing or finishing is now done and the porringer is ready to be polished.

If we choose, the handle may be riveted on, or it may be made of the same piece as the bowl by allowing enough metal where the handle is to be, to be bent back when the bowl is raised into shape.

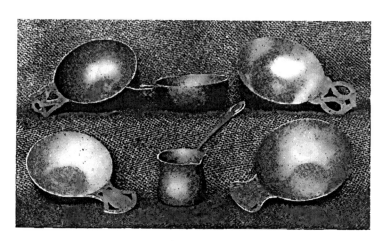

PLATE 41.

92

TRAYS OR PLATES.

Trays or plates may be made by working the bowl part over an anvil or by driving it into a sand bag until the required depth is obtained, or a form may be turned out of a block of wood and the metal driven into it. After the bowl part has been shaped it may be placed on the pitch block and the outline trued up with a chasing tool. The edge of the tray or plate may be decorated either by piercing, embossing, etching, or enameling.

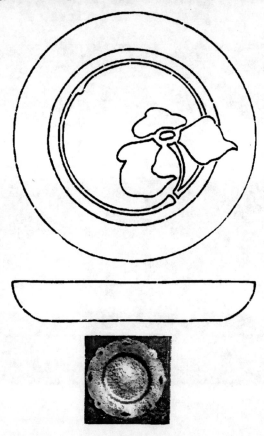

93

Chapter VIII.

INK POT.

This exercise is carried out as follows: A form is first raised like the lower part of the pot inverted, which is nothing more than a bowl so far. A hole with a diameter a little less than the diameter of the ink well is then sawed with a piercing saw in the bottom of this bowl, as at A. After this a circular piece of metal is cut equal in diameter to the top of this bowl plus $\frac{1}{4}$ of an inch, and soldered on G. By making this piece $\frac{1}{4}$ inch greater than the diameter

FIGURE 29. Dapping tools in use.

of the bowl, the soldering process becomes much easier. After the soldering is finished, the projecting edges may be filed off to the edge of the bowl. The bowl is then inverted so that it rests on its greatest diameter H, and it becomes an ink pot.

The cover, J, is made by taking a circular piece of metal and raising the sides in the same way as in the bowl except that the design calls for the sides at right angles to the

94

INK POT

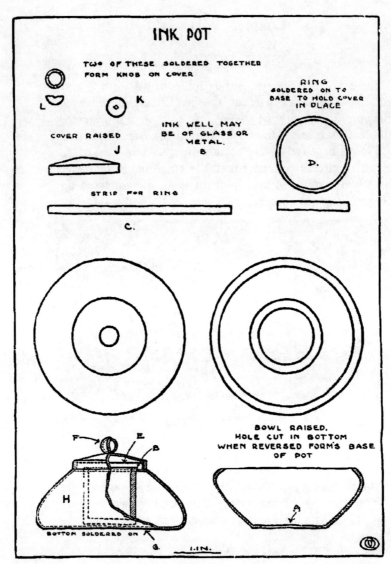

TWO OF THESE SOLDERED TOGETHER
FORM KNOB ON COVER

L

K

RING
SOLDERED ON TO
BASE TO HOLD COVER
IN PLACE

COVER RAISED

INK WELL MAY
BE OF GLASS OR
METAL.
B

J

D.

STRIP FOR RING

C.

BOWL RAISED.
HOLE CUT IN BOTTOM
WHEN REVERSED FORM'S BASE
OF POT

F

E

B

H

A

BOTTOM SOLDERED ON

G.   I IN.

PLATE 42.

PLATE 43.

96

base. The curve is obtained by placing it on a sand bag and driving it out from the inside to the required height. From a strip of copper 20 gauge and $\frac{3}{16}$ inch wide, C, make a ring, D, equal in diameter to the inside of the cover. Solder the ends of the ring together and, after shaping it over a circular stake, fit and solder it to the base, as shown in the section at E.

This keeps the cover in place. The knob, K, on the cover is made of two hemispheres, L, by use of the dapping block and tools, Figures 7 and 29. The two pieces are soldered together, filed or finished about the joint, and soldered to the cover, F. After dipping the different parts in the pickle, then washing them in clean water, and doing a little filing here and there about the joints to remove surplus solder, the ink pot is ready for finishing. This may be done by polishing, bronzing, or oxidizing.

The ink well proper should be made so that it may be removed. It should be of glass or some other material easily cleansed.

INK DOT

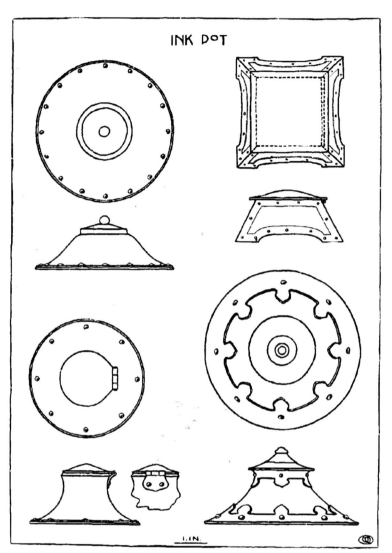

PLATE 44.

98

SEALING WAX SET.

THE WAX POT.

The wax pot is raised into shape as described in Chapter VI on raised forms. Instead of cutting the top off level, a nose is formed as shown at A, Plate 45, which will pour well. A handle is designed, sawed out, and riveted on at the position indicated at B.

THE LAMP.

The body of the lamp is made by raising a bowl to conform with the design; after cutting a hole in the bottom it is inverted, C, and the bottom is soldered on at D. A shallow cup is raised, E, a hole cut in the bottom to allow for the lamp proper, and soldered to the body. Legs as shown at F, and held together by a strip, H, are riveted to the side of the body at G; on these the wax pot rests. The lamp proper or alcohol well, which is filled with asbestos, is raised with the edges turned out, as at N, which hold it in place as shown in the section at J. The part at K serves as a burner and is placed loosely in the cup, E, allowing its removal at any time.

SEAL.

A monogram, letter or design of some sort must first be decided on. When this has been done, the design is transferred and scratched on a piece of 22 or 24 gauge copper. If the design has a right and wrong to it, the reverse should be transferred to the metal so that, when stamped, the right side will appear. The copper is then placed on the pitch and when cool enough to work upon, the lines are followed with a chasing tool, sinking them to the required depth. Care must be taken to avoid sharp edges or any undercutting, if the seal is to free itself easily from the wax. A handle for the seal may be made of wood as shown on the plate; the seal is cut and attached as shown at Section on L. M.

99

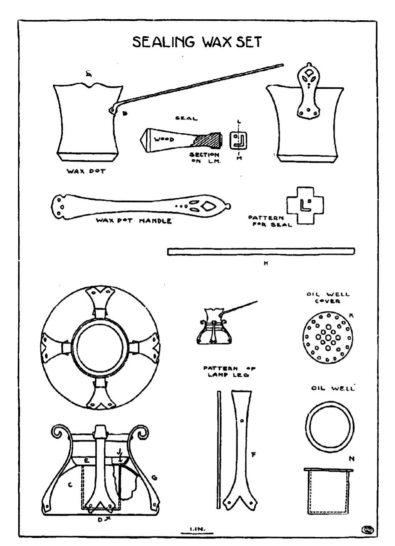

SEALING WAX SET

WAX POT

SEAL

WOOD

SECTION ON L.M.

WAX POT HANDLE

PATTERN FOR SEAL

H

OIL WELL COVER

PATTERN OF LAMP LEG

OIL WELL

1. IN.

PLATE 45.

100

WATCH FOB.

There are many ways of making watch fobs. A very simple one is made as follows: First make a drawing of the fob with some suitable pendant as at A, Plate 46. The pendant design is next transferred to a piece of 12 gauge copper, then sawed out and filed into shape. This must be done with perhaps more care than on larger work as it is to be more closely scrutinized. The parts of the fob must be made to conform with the width of the ribbon that is to be used. A bar must be made for the top, wide enough for the ribbon to be passed through and fastened. This bar is made by cutting a slot in a piece of metal of the same gauge as the pendant, or by bending a piece of wire around a piece of metal about $\frac{1}{16}$ of an inch thick and the width of the ribbon, making the ends meet in the centre of one of the long sides. If more than one of these pieces is needed, the wire is wound around the metal as many times as there are pieces required and sawed apart. The ends are then bent to come in line with each other and soldered. The piece is again placed over the metal and, with a rawhide hammer, worked into shape. The links that connect the bar and the swivel are made as all links are made. Take a piece of iron or steel wire the size required and also a piece of copper; place one end of the steel wire and one end of the copper wire in a vise so that the steel wire stands vertical. Then wind the copper wire around the steel wire spirally with as many turns as there are links required. Now take it out of the vise and slip it off the steel wire, which leaves it in the shape of a spring. Hold it with the thumb and forefinger of the left hand and, resting it against the bench pin, saw the links off with a fine saw one at a time until there are as many as needed.

WATCH FOBS

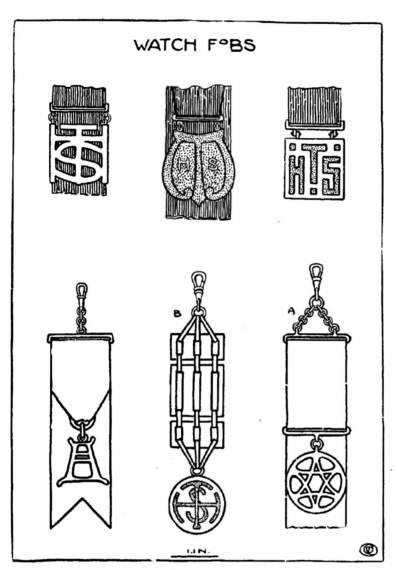

PLATE 46.

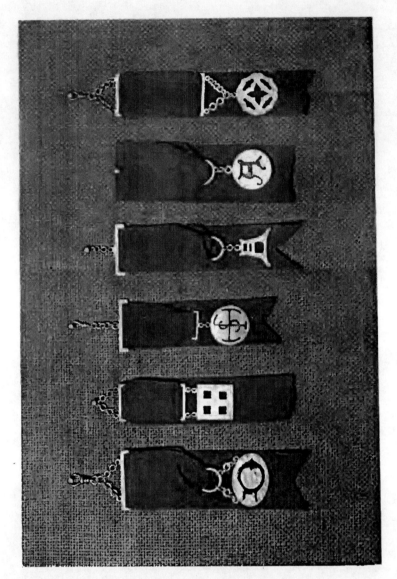

PLATE 47.

103

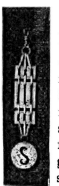

One of these links is soldered to the bar that holds the ribbon and one to the top of the pendant; the others are linked together to form the short chain at the top. To connect the pendant to the ribbon, two larger links are needed which are made in the same way as the small ones. All the links may be soldered or not. The links that are soldered to the bar and to the pendant should be filed flat a little to make the point of contact greater. This insures a more secure joint. When soldering such small pieces the charcoal block is indispensable, for depressions are easily made in it where necessary. The parts are placed on the block in position and a small mouth blow-pipe is used; with this the flame can be more delicately applied.

When the different parts are completed, they are pickled, rinsed, dried, and polished, and then put together with the ribbon.

Fobs are sometimes made entirely of metal as B, Plate 46. In this slots are sawed in three or more bars of metal which are linked together with links made from the same thickness metal as the bars. The pendant and the swivel are also connected with the same kind of links.

Chapter IX.

SPOONS, SUGAR TONGS AND TEA SCOOPS.

These exercises are easily carried out after a little experience. No steps are taken that have not already been described, except in the case of forming the bowl of the spoon. This is done by taking a piece of lead and making a depression in it the size and shape of the bowl required. A piece of hard wood is shaped on the end grain to fit the depression made in the lead. The metal is placed over the depression and the wood shape placed on top of the metal; it is then driven into the form by using a hammer. This will give the general shape of the bowl which may be trued up later by sawing and filing.

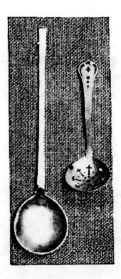

SPOONS

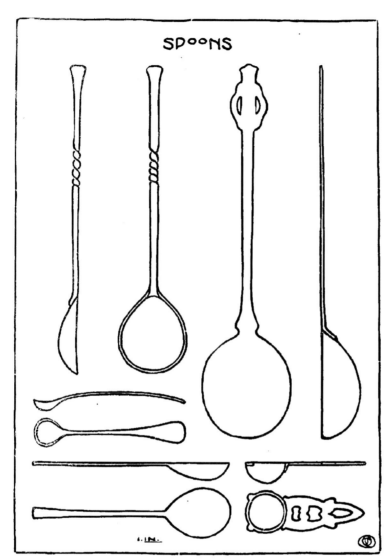

PLATE 48.

106

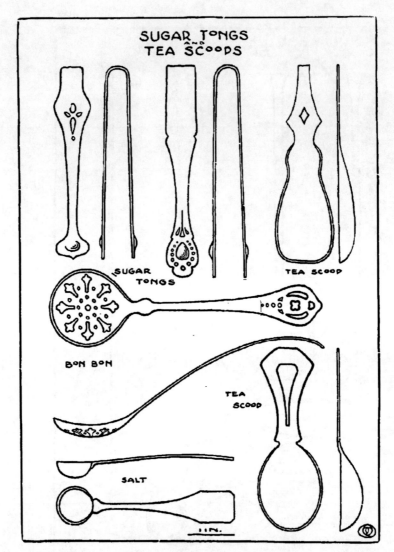

SUGAR TONGS
AND
TEA SCOOPS

SUGAR TONGS

TEA SCOOP

BON BON

TEA SCOOP

SALT

PLATE 49.

107

RIVETS.

The making of rivets is quite important as it is impossible to find in the market the variety in size and shape of head that each piece of work demands. Where rivets with a wire $\frac{1}{8}''$ or less are needed, they may be made as follows: Take a piece of iron or steel A, Plate 50, thicker than the desired length of the rivet and drill a hole through it having its diameter a little greater than the wire of the rivet. Take a piece of copper wire of the required diameter and about $\frac{1}{8}''$ longer than the thickness of the iron. Place the wire in the hole and the iron on some smooth metal surface, B. With a hammer make a burr of the wire that projects above the iron. Then reverse the iron and drive out the rivets. This gives what is shown at D. The rivet is then cut off the required length, placed in position and headed up. The head may be made conical, I, hemispherical, J, pyramidal, K, or square, L, in shape. It may be headed up simply with the hammer, or with a rivet header, M.

When necessary, the process may be reversed and the head made first; but when made in this way, a rivet block is needed to rest the head in while making the burr.

The rivet may be made more of a decorative feature by sawing out of sheet metal some suitable design as shown at P, Q, R. Drill a hole in the center the size of the rivet and then use any ordinary rivet head. Nails may be made by the same process, headed and pointed as at S and O.

RIVETS

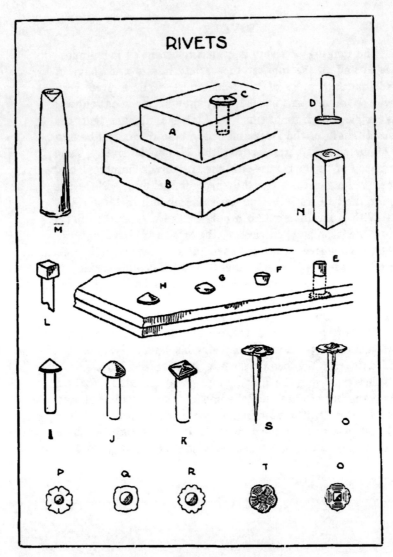

PLATE 50.

109

TO DRAW WIRE AND SMALL TUBING.

Cut a piece of copper the length required, having the width about three times the diameter of the tube that is to be made. The edges must first be made parallel by filing.

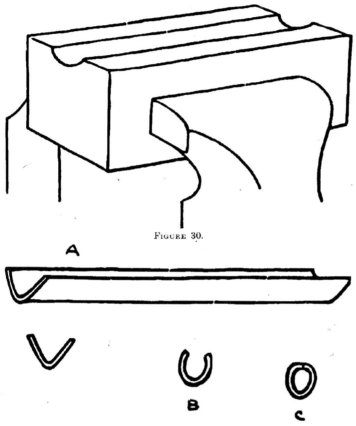

FIGURE 30.

FIGURE 31.

In a block of maple or some hard wood, with a wood file, make a groove as shown at Figure 30. Place the strip of metal over the groove and, with a somewhat pointed hammer, drive the metal into it until it takes the shape of a V. Figure 31 A. Then place it on the flat part of the block and strike on the edges with the hammer, turning them in until they meet, as at B and C.

A draw plate is then placed in the vise, Figure 32.

FIGURE 32.

After pointing the tube a little, the end is placed in one of the larger holes and drawn through. This will bring it somewhat into shape. Repeat this operation by drawing the tube through the hole the next smaller in size and so on till the tube is of the diameter required.

Wire may be drawn in the same way. Rectangular, triangular and square drawplates may be obtained as well as circular ones.

POLISHING.

To polish work, a cloth or felt buff is placed on a lathe or a polishing head. With a little cut-quick and rouge objects may be brightened by holding them against the wheel.

III

STAMPING WORK.

The marking of work so that it will be known to whom it belongs and doing it in a neat and workmanlike manner is sometimes a problem. Using a gummed label with the name written on it has been tried, but the labels frequently come off. The name has been scratched with a sharp-pointed tool, but it is not an easy thing to do and certainly does not

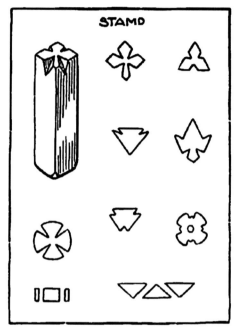

FIGURE 33.

look well. The way described below however has proved very satisfactory. Have each pupil design a little trade mark of his own, and work it out on the end of a piece of tool steel, $\frac{1}{8}$ inch or $\frac{3}{16}$ inch square, round or hexagonal. This can be done by a little filing, perhaps the use of a drill if the design should call for it, and a little emery paper to take off all sharp edges. This serves as a stamp with which he may mark all of his work. The instructor has a book with the names of the pupils, and after each name he may stamp this mark and thereby register it so that he may tell at any time to whom work belongs.

Figure 33 shows a stamp and a few suitable designs.

COLORING.

The most satisfactory color that can be given copper is a bronze which comes naturally if left to come in contact with varying atmospheres. If the object has a good polished surface in the first place the color seems to become richer as time goes on.

A color that is satisfactory in many cases is obtained in the following way:

Place in a porcelain dish and bring to a boiling heat, liver of sulphur, 1 oz., and water, 1 qt. Dip the object to be colored in this solution while hot and then rinse in clean water. This gives the object a very dark color. Take a little powdered pumice stone on a piece of cloth and rub over the surface lightly bringing the copper color to the surface where desired.

A greenish color is given copper by submitting the object to the fumes of spirits of ammonia.

Beautiful colors are obtained by heating the object to different degrees, over a gas plate, but these results are not permanent.

Chapter X.

ENAMELING.

Enamel may be applied to metal objects and add a great deal to their value and attractiveness if used sparingly. The enamels most used are transparent and opaque; the transparent reflects the color of the metal adding a great deal of life to the work, the opaque gives color on the surface only.

The process, as described in this chapter, touches but the elementary stages of the art that are within the possibilities of high school work and possibly the upper grammar grades.

Enamel may be applied by any of the following methods:

First: By covering the entire surface of the object with enamel.

Second: By using a flat wire which is bent into sections the shape of the design and soldered to the object; the wire forms partitions to receive the enamel.

Third: By cutting away the design by the use of engraving tools, making channels about $\frac{1}{32}$ of an inch deep to receive the enamel.

Fourth: By using a chasing tool either from the front or from the back of the work, forming raised or sunken partitions to receive the enamel.

The first and second methods are difficult ones, requiring a great deal of experience in handling metal and enamel to obtain satisfactory results.

The third and fourth methods are comparatively simple and are within the possibilities of those for whom this book is intended.

In the third method the design is first transferred to the object by the use of carbon paper and then made more

permanent with a scratcher. The design is cut out with
the engraving tools, Figures 6, 34 and 35, about $\frac{1}{32}$ of
an inch deep. All edges should be kept as smooth as possible and the channels should be uniform in depth. For
convenience in holding, if the work is small, it may be
fastened to a little pitch or wax spread on a block, or it may

FIGURE 34.

be placed on the pitch block as described under embossing
on page 64. The handle of the tool is held in the palm of
the hand, and the thumb, placed within an inch of the point,
serves as a guide while cutting, Figures 34 and 35. By
wriggling the tool a little from one side to the other,
greater progress is possible.

In the fourth method the design is transferred to either side
of the object. After placing it on a pitch block, depressions
may be made from the face or lines raised from the under side.

After the partitions have been formed, the object must
be thoroughly cleaned and brightened by dipping in a bath

115

of nitric acid. After dipping, which should be done quickly on account of the rapid action of the acid on the metal, it should be rinsed thoroughly in clean water. This process removes all dirt and leaves the metal bright. After this cleaning, the fingers should not touch any part of the object that is to receive the enamel.

To prepare the enamel for application it must be ground. First break it into small pieces with a hammer. To keep it from flying about, it is well to roll it up in a piece of heavy wrapping paper. It is then placed in a porclain mortar and, with a little water and a pestle, it is ground about as fine as fine sand. The water is poured off and the enamel rinsed several times in clean water until the milky substance disappears. Unsatisfactory results often come from lack of care in washing the enamel. After washing it is removed from the mortar to a small saucer by the use of a palette knife. While still wet, which allows its being spread more easily, the enamel is applied to the object with a soft hair brush.

All of the enameling suggested in this book may be done with an ordinary blow-pipe or a Bunsen burner, but more satisfactory results are obtained with a kiln.

To apply the process to a definite piece of work, the steps necessary in enameling the Stamp Box cover on Plate 24, No. 3, will be taken up. It will be assumed that the box is made, ready for the application of the design as shown on the plate. The design is first transferred to the cover and then cut away. It is cleaned with kerosene and dipped in nitric acid as before explained. After being thoroughly washed, it is ready for the enamel. In applying the enamel care must be taken not to get particles outside of the channels. After the moisture has evaporated and the enamel has been fired it settles considerably so that this must be allowed for by rounding it above the surface. After the enamel has been applied, the strip that is soldered to the under side of the cover must be protected from the heat before firing, as the temperature required for fusing the enamel is several times greater than that required for soldering. The soldering is protected by placing a paste made of yellow ochre and water about the soldered joint

FIGURE 35.

both inside and outside of the strip. The more of this clay we bank about the joint the more protection there is. When the above has been done, the object must be left in some warm place until the moisture from both the enamel and the clay is thoroughly evaporated. It is then ready for firing. If the blow-pipe or the Bunsen burner is used, take a tripod and place a piece of heavy iron netting over the top and place the object on top of the netting. The flame should always be applied to the under side. Watch the enamel as the firing goes on and when it settles and glazes the heat should be withdrawn. The object should be allowed to cool very slowly. Hurrying at this point only increases chances for accidents. If, when cool, it is found that the channels in places are not full of enamel, the object is again cleaned in the nitric acid, more enamel applied, and fired as at first. The cover is now ready to finish. The enamel may be stoned down level with the top with an emery stone, or it may be left just as it comes from the fire in the first place. If stoned down, it is necessary to fire it again just enough to give it a glazed surface.

The directions as given apply to either transparent or opaque enamel; but, in addition to the above, when transparent enamel is used, the surface to be enameled must first receive a coating of flux to retain the transparency. The flux is treated and applied just the same as the enamel already described.

The upper half of Plate 26 shows boxes treated with enamel.

CPSIA information can be obtained at www.ICGtesting.com
Printed in the USA
BVOW04s1046010615

402667BV00010B/94/P